Butterflies and Memories

Butterflies and Memories

Melisa Calcote

Butterflies and Memories

Copyright © 2024 by Melisa Calcote. All rights reserved.

No part of this publication may be reproduced, stored in a retrieval system or transmitted in any way by any means, electronic, mechanical, photocopy, recording or otherwise without the prior permission of the author except as provided by USA copyright law.

The opinions expressed by the author are not necessarily those of URLink Print and Media.

1603 Capitol Ave., Suite 310 Cheyenne, Wyoming USA 82001
1-888-980-6523 | admin@urlinkpublishing.com

URLink Print and Media is committed to excellence in the publishing industry.

Book design copyright © 2024 by URLink Print and Media. All rights reserved.

Published in the United States of America

Library of Congress Control Number: 2024915999
ISBN 978-1-68486-871-1 (Paperback)
ISBN 978-1-68486-851-3 (Digital)

26.07.24

Contents

The Awakening 1
Angel Voices 2
Be Still 3
The Church In The Country 4
Come And Follow Me 5
Come To The Cross 7
Come To The River 8
Covenant 9
Curves In The Road 10
Earth, Wind And Sky 11
Free At Last! 12
Hands Reaching Out 15
Heavens' Blessings 16
He's Everything To Me! 17
I Am The Way 18
I Believe, I Receive 19
I Cannot See God 21
I Shall Not Be Moved 22
If Time Stood Still 23
In My Father's House 24
In The Arms Of Jesus 26
Just Imagine 27
Keep Your Eyes On Jesus 29
Loving Hands 31
Mountaintop High 32
My First Love 33
One Family 34
Only Believe 35
Putting The Pieces Together 36
Running Back 37
Shepherd Of My Soul 38

The Awakening

He has awakened the depth of my soul;
Everything within me, everything I know.
The urging of the Spirit that bids me to go
In spreading the gospel of my Lord
And Savior, Jesus Christ.
To be all that I can be and all that I know
From the wisdom He imparts
Deep down in my soul.

I have this stirring deep within me, it goes far and beyond.
In the wonder of it all, through the urging of the spirit,
I have awakened to thee, O Lord!

I am very much willing to answer thy call,
To run this race that is set before me,
The race of Faith that is so fulfilling.

I want to serve you, Lord, in so many ways,
Wherever I can to show others the way
To you, my Lord and Savior.
For it is through you all things are possible
Lord, use me and guide me in all that I do,
For all the glory and honor will go to you.

Yes, there's an awakening that's happened
Deep down in my soul,
To reach out to your children, Lord,
So that others can be made whole.

Angel Voices

Angel voices I hear,
That are coming near,
Angel wings I feel,
And a chance to steal
The moment with you near me.

Most of the time I will come
Within to speak only of the truth,
To let you know that there is proof
Of His real Love for thee.
I come to you thru spiritual appearance.
Yes there is a clearance
Of something so real and true,
That speaks only to you.
You will know for sure
That what I tell you is pure,
And from the heart of my Lord.
Avoid all obstacles that will try to embrace,
For here, Satan has no place,
And that will be a trace you are connected to me.

Be Still

Walking along the sand by the sea,
The foaming water coming up to meet me,
And the coolness rushes over my feet
That calms the anxieties within me.

The seagulls are flying up overhead
As they search for food down below,
Diving into the water out into the deep and
 Catching their dinner to keep.

And staring out into the blue,
I thought for a moment that I saw you
Looking back at me.
As the sound of the ocean roars,
And the waves seem to wash over me,
I sit at the waters' edge, watching and
Waiting for a response from thee.

Then as if a soft voice uttered, "Peace, be still",
The ocean was suddenly smooth and still
At the command of my Fathers' will.
Then the message you instilled within me,
"Be still and know me,
Be still and know my Fathers' will."

The Church In The Country

It was the place of my youth,
Where the brown church stood,
Out on a country road in the hills.
Proud and tall, it stood, for it knew many years,
Served several families, from generation to generation.

It knew many pastors, and held quite a many weddings,
Christenings, Christmas plays, Easter egg hunts,
Revivals and the fellowship of God through the years.

The Great Spirit of our Holy God resides
Here at every church service and all family gatherings.
He watched us grow from toddler to teenager,
And as we matured through the years into adulthood.
And He went with each one of us as we went our separate ways;
 There was that tie that could not be broken.
For in our hearts, that always brought us back home to this
Marvelous place and time,
To where our hopes and dreams began.

Now there is a new bell tower built in, and the
Sanctuary had been remodeled through the years,
New buildings added, and a great new dining hall,
Where we gathered in God's name to praise and
Worship Him in fellowship and song.
A place I always look forward to revisiting,
Time and time again.
For family reunions and visiting old friends, and to
Worship the Lord my God in a place that I grew up in.

The brown church in the country was my first
Memory of my heritage and faith;
Where they had planted a seed, -
God watered it, and watched it grow.

Come And Follow Me

Walking by the Sea of Galilee, He called out to thee and said
'Come and follow me. And I will make you fishers of men.'

They came, they believed, they saw,
The many miracles of our Lord.
The great love and compassion that He had for others,
The patience, the caring, the giving of His heart.
They learned of His love, the passion within Him.
They walked with Him, ate with Him and
Prayed with Him through all their journeys
As they followed His example of Love
And forgiveness, and they taught the way
Of the Lord to all who would listen,
Who wanted a new life, a new purpose.

He gave them a reason for living,
How to love one another, through peace, joy,
Compassion, and forgiving.
And He told them of his Father, who is in heaven,
The one true God, for He is the Alpha,
And the Omega, the beginning and the End,
The Creator of all Life.

All He asks us today to give everything to Him,
To turn our lives over to Him, to follow Him and
Be a disciple of the Lord Jesus Christ.
For He said, 'He who believes in me shall have eternal life.'
"Come and follow me.'

Come To The Cross

Are you troubled and blue and
Don't know what to do?
Have you too many burdens to bear?

Bring it to the cross, and
Lay it there at the bottom, and just walk away.
Walk away from all that's troubling you.
Walk away from the sickness from within too.
Leave it with Jesus who died for you and me,
For He died to set us free.

Free from sin and the burden of the world.
Free from the troubles when we don't know what to do,
Free from the guilt and pain in your life.
Bring it to the cross, and leave it there.
Where we can be reborn in the Spirit of God,
And be forgiven of our sins too.

Remember, He was wounded for our transgressions,
He was bruised for our iniquities.
He came to earth to bring us salvation.
Come to the cross, bring all your burdens,
And leave them at Jesus feet.
For God will never leave us nor forsake us
In our hour of need.

Come To The River

Come to the river
Come let us gather
In the shade of the cover He gives.

Let the waters flow over
As I go under,
As He takes away my sins
And I receive the new life He gives.
For as my heart opens to be filled with
His Spirit, For it is through Him that we live.

For through Jesus, our Lord,
He gives through redemption,
Forgiveness of our sins.
And He gives us the great commission
As we go out into the world
To spread the Good News of His Name.

Come to the river, Come let us gather
And renew our commitment in Him.

Covenant

I am the Lord, I have called Him in righteousness,
He is a Covenant to the people,
A Light to the Nations.

"Through him, the eyes of the blind will open,
The sick will be healed, and
I will set the captives free.
They will know that I am their God.
I am the Lord, indeed.
For all former things have passed away
And the new is here to stay."

Sing to the Lord a new song,
For his grace endures forever.
Sing to the Lord a new song, For it is through this endeavor
That we have eternal life.
Let the seas roar and all that is in it,
The coastlands and inhabitants.
Let the mountains be made low
By His mighty hand, as
He protects His people with
Whom He keeps this covenant
Of His almighty plan.

Isaiah 42:6-11

Curves In The Road

Life has thrown so many curves in our lives today,
That you sometimes feel you don't know which way to turn.

Satan's good at his trick of the trade,
He thinks he can win you over.
But there's one thing for sure I know,
I'm glad of the decision I made,
That I've surrendered everything to my Lord,
And I know for sure, my heart, he will guard.

So even though there may be curves in the road,
Hills to go over, and dark valleys to go through,
My Lord will be with me to look over
And protect me, and carry me through.

Earth, Wind And Sky

Wind,
Music of the earth,
Let me grasp it in my hand
And hold it there for a while
Before it goes away,
Away to another hand
Another land.
To where it might come back again,
The hand of the earth that
Stands like a mountain,
And has molds in its dirt
That holds the rain.
Rain that falls from the
Clouds that float up in the sky.
Sky,
Space that's a part of the universe.

Free At Last!

All alone she sits and wonders
Where did she go wrong?
For around her are these strangers
Who are also so alone, in their own little world,
Wallowing in their own guilt, and
Praying for forgiveness for the things they had done.

No one to turn to, she thought,
Who would understand, what a mixed up world this is?
How can she go back, with what she knew she had done?
Can she go on with this thorn, that won't let go?

Finally, turning to the Lord in desperation,
She releases everything to Him,
In hopes of restoration of her soul
And he does say to her, "It's okay, my child".
I know it's hard to run away
But I Love you, my child,
And you can make it through me."

Our God is a loving God,
Who does want us to come home,
Like the father of the prodigal son,
Who will accept us and forgive us
No matter what we have done.
He waits patiently, with outreached hands
To nurture us, cleanse us,
And bring us back into his fold. And yet it came time,
The day she went back,
Only to say good-bye for the last time.
Letting go and saying good-bye to the past.

No more headaches, no more drugs.
Finally, set free from the pain, -
The worry, the guilt, and the shame,
for God had set her free at last.

Hands Reaching Out

When a hand reaches out for another,
It's looking for the comfort of someone dear;
Someone they could confide in.

A hand reaches out for compassion,
Brotherly love, and understanding.
A hand reaches for someone
Who's reaching back for a Friend.

When the hands of people come together,
They tie together a bond of friendship and the
 Love of God that cannot be broken.

I'm reaching out looking for someone
Who's reaching back to me.
Just a Friend that I need to walk
With me along this rocky road.

I'm reaching out to you, my Friend,
Who will reach out to hold my hand.
Let me show you Jesus, who He is to me.
How he's changed my life, and
What he's done for me.
How he's brought me to this point in time,
And how much He's blessed me through all eternity
Let me tell you how much he cares for you and me.

I'm not just reaching out to you, my Friend.
I want to tell you WHO Jesus is.

Heavens' Blessings

Heavens' blessings are stored in you,
God's glory lives in you.

"God, who commanded the light to shine
Out of darkness and sparks fire into our hearts
To give us the light of the knowledge of
The glory of God in the face of Jesus Christ."

He'll give us wisdom and guard our spirit
The darkness, we will not fear it.
He'll keep the glory shining through
That's there for me and you.
We'll walk in Love- Love of God,
And love for each other
Down this path we trod.
He'll keep us on the right track
In His Glory will not lack
For He is the Light-
The light that shines thru us
As One – we live in harmony.

Heavens' Blessings are there for us
For where our heart is, is the treasure of God.
A treasure worth waiting for.

He's Everything To Me!

He is the Advocate, the Almighty, our King
Like the gentleness of a doe
With her fawn beside a natural spring.

He is the Alpha, Omega, the great I AM.
He was brought into this world,
- The Son of God.
- He is the lamb.
He is the Author, the Finisher,
The Beginning and the End
Through all in all,
He's my Best Friend.

He is my Comforter, my Counselor
He is always there to console my soul
He gives me strength to endure
To remain in him is my goal.

He's everything to me!

I Am The Way

I am the Way, the Truth, and the Life.

I AM the way, -the only way to salvation.
When you ask in my name,
I will always answer.
Through me, there is eternal life.
I AM the Truth that will set you free.

Free from guilt and your old life of sin.
My Father has forgiven you,
He will cleanse you, redeem you, and
Set you in the right direction
He will purify you and make you whole.
He will change your heart and
Give you a brand new start.

I AM the Life and Light of the world.
I am the light that shines in the darkness
To help show you the way out,
And the way back to my Father, -Yahweh.

He's waiting for you to open your heart,
To let Him come in and be a part of your life.
For He stands at the door of your heart
Waiting for you to welcome Him in.

All you have to do is ask,
And it shall be given,
Seek and ye shall find.
Knock and the door
Shall be opened unto you.
Matthew 7:7-8

I Believe, I Receive

I Believe, I Receive
Power in His name.
I Believe, I Receive is what
He taught me to proclaim.

For he pointed me toward the scriptures
Which proclaims his powerful word.
Where he said whatever I should ask in his name,
That I shall receive.

So I claim the Victory in all things in my life.
I stand against all evil with the Power of His Name.
I no longer have any worry or any kind of strife,
For he gives me the power-
Power in his Name.

It is plain to see that Jesus is the Way.
He not only is the doorway,
But He is the gift of Life.
He lives today for you and me
So we can all be set free.
Through him, all things are possible,
 Because Jesus Christ is the Way.
I walk along His path to true eternal life,
For it is in God I wish to stay.
I Believe, I Receive
Victory in Jesus Name every day of my life,
Yesterday, Today, and Tomorrow.
For I know in Jesus, there is no sorrow,
He brings me the joy of things to come,
And blessings upon blessings
In every little way.

I Believe, I Receive
Power in His Name.
I Believe, I Receive everything
He has promised to me.

I Cannot See God

I cannot see God but I know that He's there.
He's deep down in my heart,-
The Spirit within me,
In the people I meet, and the birds in the air.

I cannot see God,
But I see Him in different people,
People like you.

I cannot see God,
I don't know what He looks like,
I only know that He's old, yet
Young at heart, and knows everything about us.
He created us- you and me.
He created the earth, the skies,
The seas, - the deep blue.

I see Him in so many things around me,
In the trees, the flowers and
I feel Him in the cool breeze.

I cannot see God, but I know that He's there.
He's the Father, the Son, and the Holy Ghost.

He's my comforter, my strength and my shield.
He protects me with loving care and
Holds me gently in His arms.
My Lord, Jesus Christ, intercedes for me
That I may continuously be in touch with Him.

I Shall Not Be Moved

He is the Rock on which I stand
He is the source of the great plan
For eternal life through Jesus Christ,
So I run this race for the prize.

I shall not be moved.
He is my strength and my salvation.
He is the reason there is celebration.
No, I shall not be moved.

My soul waits patiently
For the sound of His voice,
For when He speaks to me,
My heart leaps and rejoices
In the Love he has for me.
I shall not be moved.

If Time Stood Still

If the colors of the rainbow
Shone as bright as the sun,
Then all around would notice
How much there is to be done.
For just maybe they would notice
The brilliance of His glory;
And somehow realize
There are so many more souls
That don't really know Him

If time stood still,
Would we notice it?
Not knowing that He's giving us time?
TIME - to really get to know Him,
Before time runs out.

The Lord is being patient,
And all the saints are praying
For each and everyone, -
That we will soon accept Him
Into our hearts to stay,
For He's waiting with open arms
To welcome us home today.

In My Father's House

In my Father's house
There are many rooms
That are built for you and me.
And there are streets paved with gold
Where we will walk within the Father's fold,
As from the scriptures we're foretold.

In my Father's kingdom, Where our family waits,
Anticipating in our arrival to celebrate
As one big family reunion;
When we come before the banquet table
And come together in communion;
Where we shall gather in unity.

And there is a banquet for us that awaits
For when we reach heaven's gates
On that grand finale day!

The tables are set,
Preparations are made,
All the angels anticipate this glorious day
Everyone will be ready and arrayed
In robes of gold and displayed
For the glory of our Lord
To whom this day reigns.

For Jesus came from the stable
Into the pages of our history,
And brought to those who are able
And who chose to believe, into Christianity.
Yet, now He Lives today in my Father's House,

Anticipating the moment in time,
And looking forward to His return
Into the future of the great sublime
To bring us home to where
We'll live in one accord within my Father's House.

In The Arms Of Jesus

In the arms of Jesus...
Is where I long to be
Where He gives me reassurance
When I come to Him on bended knee.
For in His presence, is where I long to
Stay, for it is there when He brings me peace,
Where He takes all cares away,
Worries of the world seem to cease
As I come to Him in prayer.

In the arms of Jesus...
There is satisfaction
And fulfillment of my soul,
For He takes away all distractions.
In him, I am made complete and whole.

In the arms of Jesus.
Where the urging of the Spirit
Leads me on a daily basis.
Where He calms the raging sea.
It is like being in an oasis,
And time stands still for me.

For in the arms of Jesus...
Is where I will stay
He is my everything, and my ALL.
It is my destiny to be in the
Arms of Jesus, my Lord.

Just Imagine

Let's imagine for a moment when Jesus was born,
 He wanted to reach down and hold him.
Just imagine how He wanted to comfort him
When others did not accept him.

Just imagine how He felt when others ridiculed him,
How our Father in Heaven wanted to reach out to
Put His arms around him.
Just imagine how He wanted to be there for him physically,
As well spiritually, when he was learning and growing in
The knowledge of the Law and the Torah.

Just imagine for a moment, how He felt when his son was on the cross
 And even though He knew the outcome,
It all crushed Him on the inside, having to watch him go through
All the pain and suffering, to pay for the price of many.

Just imagine - at that brief moment,
When He had to turn away and cried a flood of tears.
Yet, on the day Jesus rose from the dead
-His heart rejoiced and was eager to welcome him home with open
Arms into the heavenly realm that was appointed to him.

And yet, the many times when our Father wanted to be there for him-
Instead, He sent others in His place;
To nurture him as he grew, to teach him the ways of the law,
To show him the love and patience of a mother,
To reach out to him as a sister or brother,
To abide in him in the spirit, and
To guide and protect him through His Love.

So as you can see, if you can imagine
How much our Father in heaven was actually

There for Jesus, imagine, if you will, and
Hold tight to the reality of His presence in your life.
The many ways He has sent messages to you,
Through so many people, in so many ways,
Of how much He loves you.
And yes, He is the Father of the prodigal son or daughter,
Who waits patiently and earnestly for His children to come home.
Yes, He knows what it's like to pace the floor,
Worrying about His children, waiting to hear from them,
Wondering how they're doing and He sees how we're doing.
And yet, He reaches down into our lives, touches our hearts and
Souls, through the many people He places in our paths to help us grow
In His Love and show us the way back home to Him.
Imagine and hold true the Great and Wonderful Love He has for you!

Keep Your Eyes On Jesus

Keep your eyes on Jesus,
No matter the pace.
Keep your eyes on Jesus,
Throughout the entire race.

Lean on His everlasting arms,
Where there is strength and consolation.
 Lean on His enduring Love,
For he is the sure foundation.

Keep your eyes on Jesus,
Who brings peace from within,
Who calls us to repentance,
Who forgives us of our sin.

Keep your eyes on Jesus,
Keep your Faith strong
For through our Lord and Savior,
You'll never ever go wrong.

Loving Hands

How we use our hands
And in how we impart,
We will come to understand
The love of the human heart.

Let us not push away
But to welcome them in,
And let no one be led astray.
Let us not be angry with fists
But to shake and have mercy;
And take the opportunity we might miss
In showing that we care.
Let voices not be raised in frustration
But to communicate and agree
And not be led in temptation
Instead have faith in thee.
Do not turn from those who suffer
But approach with loving care
To stand in to be a buffer
As you come together in prayer.

Let us Love one another as God Loves us
And be the kind and gentle brother
As we reach out in loving care.

Mountaintop High

I saw Him standing there, though it seemed so bright and fair
And the glory of the Lord shown all around as the prophets
Appeared there with Him.

What was this? What's going on? What a glory it was to be in
The presence of my Lord. Within the brilliance of
the glory of The Lord, we saw them talking. What were they
talking about?
What were they saying? Was this for us to see?
To know how real He is to me?

Then we heard a voice from heaven saying, "This is my Son,
Whom I Love, with him I am well pleased. Listen to him!"

Bowing down on the ground in fear, we worshipped Him with
Reverence and awe. But then as we looked up, no one was there
But my Lord, as He said, "Do not be afraid."

What a glory it was to be in the presence of the prophets, to be
Within the supernatural realm of the Almighty God, and to hear
His voice booming from the heavens. Jesus is real.
He is very real in my life.

Sometimes, things happen that make us realize how great the
Lord is working in miraculous ways in our own journey
He brings us to the mountaintop experience, where we can
Receive His Spirit and all the blessings He wishes to bestow on us,
Before sending us out into the world. When we experience
The glory of the Lord, He prepares us for conquering all
Situations that may come against us in our daily lives.
Therefore, take the mountain top experience with you.
Hold on to it for wherever you go or wherever you are,
You will be reminded that God is with you always.

My First Love

I have returned to my first Love,
Jesus, the lover of my soul.
Through Him, there is salvation.
For I'm complete through redemption, He's the lover of my soul.
No more wandering, or
Wondering which way to go.
For my Faith is built on Jesus Christ Who is the cornerstone.
He's the rock of my salvation,
The rock on which I stand.
For there is joy and celebration
As I'm bound for the Promised Land. Serving Him is my destiny
That I remain in communion with Him. For He's Jesus, my first Love
Now, and through all eternity.

One Family

Come take a walk with me to a place
And time of peaceful tranquility.
Where the flowers bloom and sweet songs
Of the birds are heard.
Where there is no more pain and no more sorrow,
For the Lord will wipe away our tears.

And he will give us a new song to sing,
A new reason to praise his Holy name.
For he will take away our fears and
Replace it with Joy and Thanksgiving.

Where He has prepared for us a place in his Kingdom
- The New Jerusalem.
A place for you and me where Jews and Gentiles alike
will share the Love of God as one family

Where we will together in unity
Praise the God of our Fathers
With sweet music everywhere.

Come take a walk with me, hold my hand and
Let the Love of God continue in us.
For we are his people, Jews and Gentiles alike,
One Family.

Only Believe

We take life one step at a time, one day at a time
Although times may seem tough,
God is always there to guide us through.
He will never leave us nor forsake us.
For it is through Jesus that we can do all things,
With the power of His glory inside us,
To guard and guide us in all that we do.

For the power of the Holy Spirit will
Show us the way.
He will give us wisdom and understanding
And the strength to stand through all
Situations in life.

Only believe and accept His Love and overcoming glory
That will shine in you and through you.
Only believe and be willing to be a beacon
That glows in the darkness for others to see
To show them the way.

If we only believe in the One true and loving God,
One day at a time, one step at a time,
Will He help us grow in His everlasting Love.

For God is Love, and Love is of God.
Let us Love one another as He Loves us.
Only Believe.

Putting The Pieces Together

Some days are good, some days are bad,
Then the days come what may
Of uncertainty in any way
To where the last piece
Of the puzzle fits in

I'm still letting go of the past
And the "what might have been,"
Still wonder sometimes
Exactly where do I fit in?

I've put together the puzzle
A little bit at a time,
Placing my Faith in God,
Accepting Jesus into
my Heart, soul, and mind.

And now the last piece seems to be
The dwelling of His Spirit
To be led into His presence,
Not just to feel it, but to know it,
That he's always within me.

Always healing and fulfilling
Every one of my needs,
For where the glory of the Lord is,
I will follow where he leads.

Running Back

Walking down the road,
Trying to run away from the past,
Looking for a way to go -
To get back to where she belonged.
Don't want to turn back
Or go back to where the pain began.
Don't want the hurt that she felt inside.
Don't need it any more.
Tired of hurting, tired of crying
Down deep inside.
Waiting -just waiting for the chance
To know what real Love is,
And to embrace it in God's Love.
And God came down and filled
The emptiness in the pit of her soul
Through His healing, He made her whole."

She searched and she wandered through the wilderness of life.
Wondering how in the world could he accept me as I am.
Thinking of all the wrongs she knew she had done,
Sinking deeper within her soul,
Praying, Lord, please forgive me for what I've done.

"Running back to my Father, here I am
Staying close beneath his fold.
I will never leave his side,
For in him I will reside.
I'm running into my Fathers' arms
Where I know there is Love.
He has filled that empty hole inside,
He has made me complete and whole.

Shepherd Of My Soul

He is the Shepherd of my soul,
He leads me through paths of righteousness
That will make me whole.
He brings peace into my life, and
Brings me into his presence with thanksgiving,
And into his gates with praise.
He brings joy into my heart
That renews my spirit that will
Make me complete in His Love.
For through Him, He restores me
In my body, mind and soul.

He is my Shepherd, my Lord, and my all.
For He leads me toward the right
Road towards perfection for my soul.

www.ingramcontent.com/pod-product-compliance
Lightning Source LLC
LaVergne TN
LVHW021742060526
838200LV00052B/3417